Pretend to work and I'll pretend to pay you.

Don't repeat yourself. I ignored you the first time.

You are not a real boss until you've trained your team to shoulder your responsibilities.

Today's agenda: Building my empire.

Information is power.

There are no stupid questions...
Just stupid people. ???

I'll review a raise, after _____
(Insert non-committal situation here)

There's no "I" in team, but there's a "me".

I like work. I can sit and look at it for hours.

I'm not arguing, I'm just explaining why I am right.

"Thrilled" to be here.

Today is
"bring your boss food" day!

Break time is for wimps!

Today's mood is brought to you by stupidity.

Sorry for what I said before I had my coffee!

Bring your problems here!

First job of the day, coffee time!

Emails? There's a meeting for that!

Bullshit time!

Bullshit time over!

Schedule your sicknesses around your deadlines!

I don't have the time or the crayons to explain!

Great work = More work

**Repeat after me:
I will not screw up!**

CEO of delegation

I know it was your idea but it was my idea to use your idea in the first place.

I am not bossy. I just know what you should be doing.

Teamwork = Never taking the blame yourself!

Boss: Someone who never gets tired of giving you jobs.

I didn't say it was your fault. I said I was going to blame it on you.

I speak languages:
English, profanity, sarcasm and bullshit.

Boss' workplace strategies:
1. When in charge, ponder
2. When in trouble, delegate
3. When in doubt, mumble

Teamwork: A lot of people doing what I say.

I'm the boss because I can make quick decisions on who to delegate work to.

Be happy in your own time, sweat on company time.

Definition of Boss:

Someone who is early when you are late and late when you are early.

Chaos, panic, & disorder - my work here is done.

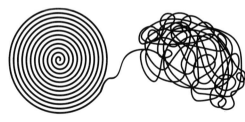

Don't say thank you, that time can be spent on other jobs.

Due to the current workload, the light at the end of the tunnel has been turned off until further notice.

Everyone brings joy to the office. Some when they enter. Some when they leave.

Sometimes, the best part of my job is that the chair swivels.

I wake up with a smile on my face every morning.
Then idiots happen.

Ring leader of the circus.

To save time, let's just assume I'm right!

Golden rule in the workplace: The boss' jokes are always funny.